# NEURO LINGUISTIC PROGRAMMING

21 DAYS COURSE

PAILA RAVI SANKAR

Made with ♥ on the Notion Press Platform
www.notionpress.com

*"To my parents, Words can hardly describe my thanks and appreciation to you. You have been my source of inspiration, support, and guidance. You have taught me to be unique and determined, to believe in myself, and to always persevere. I am truly thankful and honored to have you as my parents."*

# Contents

# Contents

# Foreword

NLP is the practice of understanding how people organise their thinking, feeling, language and behaviour to produce the results they do. NLP provides people with a methodology to model outstanding performances achieved by geniuses and leaders in their field. NLP is also used for personal development and for success.

A key element of NLP is that we form our unique internal mental maps of the world as a product of the way we filter and perceive information absorbed through our five senses from the world around us.

**What does NLP do? -NLP Applications**

Change and self development(Transformational Science)

Change work

Education

Training

Sales

Leadership

Marketing

Therapy

NLP is used as a method of personal development through promoting skills, such as self-reflection, confidence, and communication.

Practitioners have applied NLP commercially to achieve work-orientated goals, such as improved productivity or job progression.

More widely, it has been applied as a therapy for psychological disorders, including phobias, depression, generalised anxiety disorders or GAD, and post-traumatic stress disorder or PTSD.

CHAPTER ONE

# NLP Introduction

Neuro Linguistic Programming began its life early in the 1970s when an Associate Professor from the University of California, Santa Cruz, John Grinder, teamed up with an undergraduate Richard Bandler. Both men had a fascination with human excellence which charted a path for them to model the behavioural patterns of selected geniuses.

Modelling is the core activity in NLP and is the process of extricating and replicating the language structure and behavioural patterns of an individual who is excellent at a given activity.

Grinder and Bandler began their NLP quest by modelling three people, Fritz Perls, Virginia Satir and Milton Erickson. These geniuses were outstanding as professional agents of change, working in the domain of therapy. All three geniuses, Perls, Satir and Erickson performed their magic from a perspective of unconscious excellence. The geniuses did not present Grinder and Bandler with a conscious description of their behaviour. The modellers (Grinder and Bandler) unconsciously absorbed the patterning inherent in the geniuses and then provided a description.

With little direct knowledge of each of the geniuses speciality and little knowledge of the field of psychotherapy, on the whole, Grinder and Bandler over a two-year period set out with enthusiasm bordering on fervour, to explicate selected portions of the geniuses' behaviour. They coded the results of their work in language-based models using the patterns of transformational grammar as the descriptive vocabulary. Through NLP Modelling Grinder and Bandler made explicit the tacit skills of the geniuses and NLP was born.

The company that Grinder and Bandler were keeping in these heady days of the 1970s was a melting pot of enquiring minds seeking an investigation into human behaviour. John Grinder was an associate professor at the University of California, Santa Cruz and Richard Bandler was a fourth-year undergraduate student. The world-renowned anthropologist Gregory Bateson had joined the faculty at Kresge College, and such was Bateson's interest in Grinder and Bandler's collaboration that he introduced Grinder and Bandler to Milton Erickson. Bateson provided support, and feedback and his enthusiasm are in part captured in his introduction to the book Structure of Magic where he states "John Grinder and Richard Bandler have done something similar to what my colleagues and I attempted fifteen years ago."

In 1975 Grinder and Bandler presented the first two NLP models to the world in the volumes "Structure of Magic I and II." The volumes published by the respected publishing house "Science and Behaviour Books inc" put NLP on the map and interest in the new field of NLP spread quickly. People in fields related to communication, behaviour and change sought to learn how they too could get amazing results when doing change work. Grinder and Bandler willingly offered training courses in the application of their models. The training courses Bandler and Grinder conducted - proved that the NLP models were transferable to others, meaning the learners could use the NLP models successfully in their own work.

**NEURO LINGUISTIC PROGRAMMING:**

**•NEURO(Thinking Part)**

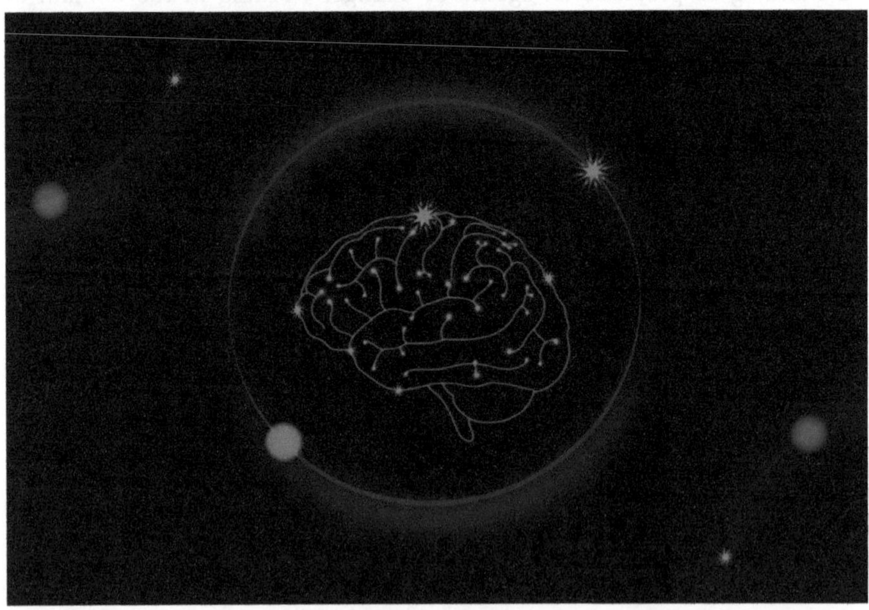

The mind and how we think. Our nervous system, the mental pathway of our five senses.

**•LINGUISTIC- (Verbal/Non-Verbal)**

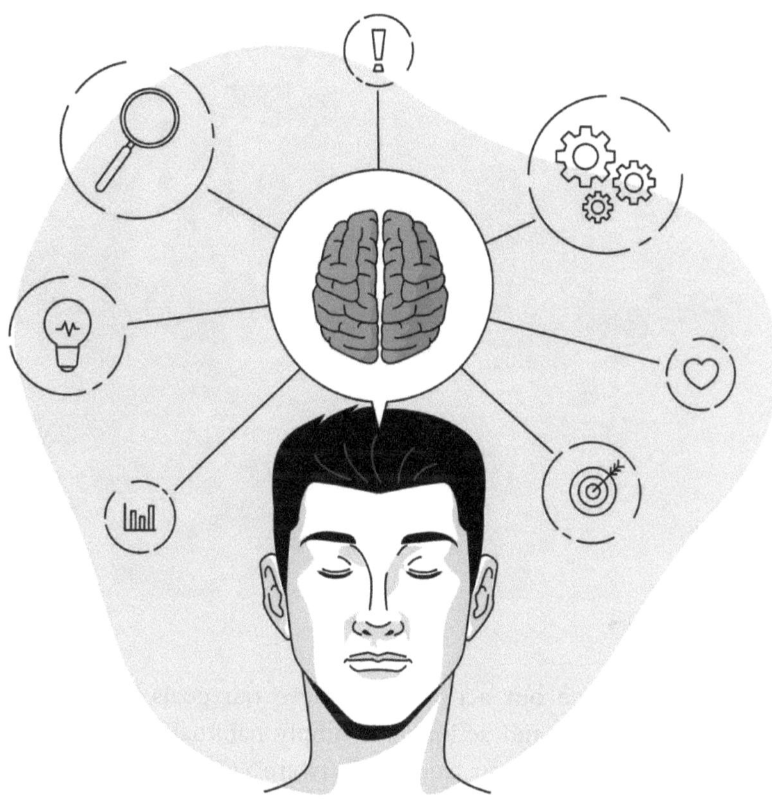

How we use language and how it (Specific words and phrases) mirror our mental world and affect us. Linguistics also refer to our "silent language" i.e. Our nonverbal behaviour like our postures, gestures, beliefs and habits that reveal our thinking style.

**•PROGRAMMING-(Pattern)**

How we sequence our actions to achieve our goals. It suggests that our thoughts, feelings and actions are simply habitual problems that can be changed by upgrading our "mental software". (Word "programming" is borrowed from computer science).

CHAPTER TWO

# Presuppositions

The principles which form the foundation of NLP have been modelled from key people who consistently produced superb results, as well as from systems theory and natural laws. We know these as "The Presuppositions of NLP"

As well as a set of powerful skills, NLP is a philosophy and an attitude that is useful when your goal is excellence in whatever you do. We invite you to discover what happens in your life if you simply 'act as if the following statements are true...

- Have respect for the other person's model of the world. (We are all unique and experience the world in different ways. Everyone is an individual and has their own special way of being).
- The map is not the territory. (People respond to their 'map' of reality, not to reality itself. How people make sense of the world around them is through their senses and from their own personal experience; this means that each individual's perception of an event is different).
- Mind and body form a linked system. (Your mental attitude affects your body and your health and, in turn, how you behave).
- If what you are doing isn't working, do something else. (Flexibility is the key to success).
- The choice is better than no choice. (Having options can provide more opportunities for achieving results).
- We are always communicating. (Even when we remain silent, we are communicating. Non-verbal communication can account for a large proportion of a message).
- The meaning of your communication is the response you get. (While your intention may be clear to you, it is the other person's interpretation and response that reflects your effectiveness. NLP teaches you the skills

and flexibility to ensure that the message you send equals the message they receive).

- There is no failure, only feedback. (What seemed like failure can be thought of as success that just stopped too soon. With this understanding, we can stop blaming ourselves and others, find solutions and improve the quality of what we do).
- Behind every behavior, there is a positive intention. (When we understand that other people have some positive intention in what they say and do (however annoying and negative it may seem to us), it can be easier to stop getting angry and start to move forward).
- Anything can be accomplished if the task is broken down into small enough steps. (Achievement becomes easier if activities are manageable; NLP can help you learn how to analyze what needs to be done and find ways to be both efficient and effective).

CHAPTER THREE

# State

**What is a state?**

--A sum total of neuro-physiological processes at a given point of time.

--It is our way of being at any moment.

--It is sum total of thoughts + emotions + physical energy

--It is just your 'mood' at any point of time

**Two components of a STATE**

a. Physiology.

b. Personal Internal Representation(Focus & words)

States can be Resourceful or Unresourceful.

**Resourceful states:** confidence, happiness, delightfulness, concentration, ecstasy, decision making, love, flexibility, playfulness etc.,

**Unresourceful states:** fear, phobia, trauma, sadness, guilt, discomfort, confusion,depression, frustration, etc.,

**How do we create a STATE?**

**How do we perceive the world?**

Through five senses

i.e. through

See (Visual learning)

Hear (Auditory learning)

Touch (kinesthetic learning)

Smell (olfactory learning)

Taste (gustatory learning)

**Remember:** We don't perceive the world as it is, we delete, distort or generalise before we perceive it and then create our inner representation.

**How to control our mind?(10 seconds)**

Changing your state(*Unresourceable state to Resourceable state*)

State= *Focus+Words+Physiology*

**Procedure:**

Power pose, Think about the happiest moment in your life, Say the words to yourself “I am born to succeed”, “I am doing it,I deserve it”.

CHAPTER FOUR

# The NLP Communication Model

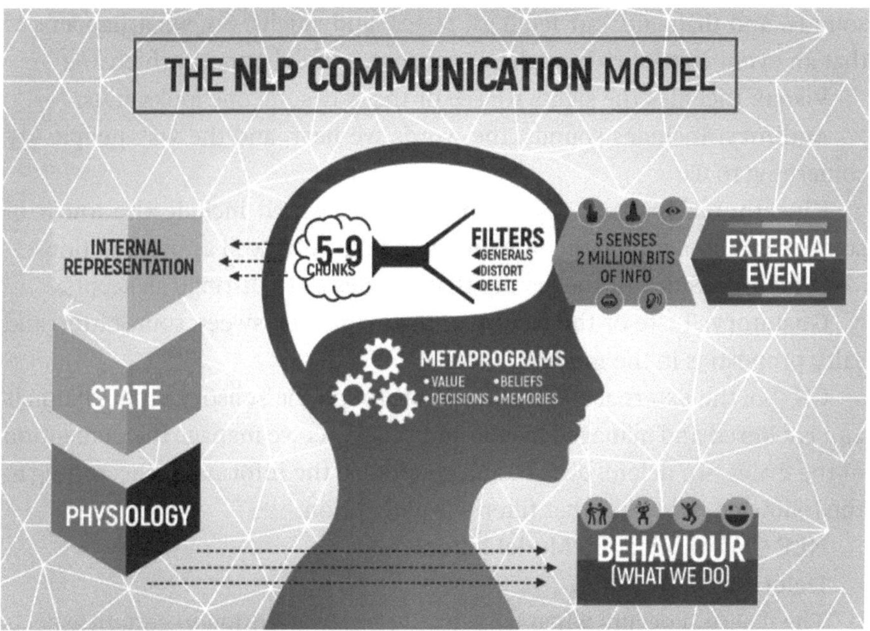


Originally conceived and developed by John Grinder and Richard Bandler, NLP or Neuro Linguistic Programming began as a model of how we communicate and interact with ourselves and others. The NLP communication model explains how we process the information that comes in from outside us and what we do with it inside.

In NLP, we believe that "The map is not the territory," so the internal representations that we make about an outside event are not essentially the event itself. What happens is that there is an external event and we run that event through our internal processing. We make an Internal Representation (I/R) of that event. The I/R of the event then combines with physiology to create a state. The word "State" refers to the internal emotional state of the individual, happy, sad, motivated, etc.

Did you ever notice that people treat their perceptions differently? Some people have to "see" certain relationships between things, whereas others have to have it explained or so they can "hear it". Still, others have to "get a grasp or a feeling" for the relationships. This is the essence of the NLP Communication Model.

The words, Internal Representation (I/R) include our internal pictures, sounds, and dialogue, our feelings, tastes, and smells. So, what happens is that an event comes in through our sensory input channels, which are:

**Visual:** Includes the sights we see or the way someone looks at us;

**Auditory:** Includes sounds, the words we hear, and the way people say something to us;

**Kinesthetic:** Internal or external feelings which include the touch of someone or something, the pressure, and texture as well as our emotions;

**Olfactory:** Smell or the faculty that enables us to distinguish scents;

**Gustatory:** Taste or the faculty of distinguishing sweet, sour, bitter, and salty properties in the mouth.

OK. So, the external event comes in through the sensory input channels and is filtered and managed by our neurology. As we manage the perception of the event, we delete, distort, and generalize the information according to the following processes that filter our perception.

**NLP Communication Model Filters**

**Deletion:**

The deletion occurs when we selectively pay attention to certain aspects of our experience and not others. We overlook or omit others. Without deletion, we would be faced with too much information. Maybe you already are overloaded with information and you feel like you have too much.

**Distortion:**

Distortion occurs when we misrepresent reality by making shifts in our experience of sensory data. In Indian philosophy, there is a well-known story of distortion in the rope versus snake analogy. A man walking along the road sees what he believes to be a snake and yells "SNAKE." However, upon arriving at that place he is relieved as he discovers that what he sees is only a piece of rope.

Distortion is an important component of the NLP Communication Model and can be used to motivate ourselves. Motivation can happen when we actually misrepresent, change or garble the material that has come into our neurology. The information has been changed by one of our filtering systems.

**Generalization:**

Finally, comes generalization, and here we draw global conclusions based on one or two experiences. Do you know someone who has one experience and forms an opinion about all similar experiences? EG: “I hate all Indian music because I have heard Ravi Shankar and did not like it.”

Usually, the conscious mind can only handle seven (plus or minus 2) pieces of information at any given time. It gets overloaded. So, we tend to oversimplify, make decisions, and set attitudes based on insufficient information. It’s critical to understand this in terms of the larger NLP Communication Model. Generalization is very common in the world today. Everybody does it. It is a result of digital information causing information overload and taking over sensibility.

Of course, we all know many people can’t even handle this number, and I know you know people who can only process “1 (plus or minus 2).” How about you?

Try this: Can you name more than 7 products in a given product category, say cigarettes? Most people will be able to name 2, maybe 3 products in a category of low interest and usually no more than 9 in a category of high interest. There is a reason for this.

If we did not actively delete information all the time, we would end up with much too much information coming in. In fact, you may have even heard psychologists say that if we were simultaneously aware of all of the sensory information that was coming in, we would go crazy. That is why we filter the information.

At its best, generalization is one of the ways that we learnâ€”- taking the information we have and drawing broad conclusions about the meaning of those conclusions. So, the question is, when two people have the same stimulus, why do they not have the same response? The answer is, that we delete, distort, and generalize the information from the outside that comes in from our senses

We do this filtering on the basis of conditioning: we compare and connect ('mapping') the flow of sensory information (previous phase) with previously coded representations before we label it a linguistic description (we can do this with 7 +/- 2 chunks do information simultaneously (126 bits per second).

That conditioning consists of:

Memories

Beliefs

Values

Decisions

Meta programs

CHAPTER FIVE

# Modalities And Submodalities

Modalities are built through our preferred representational system. Everything you experience is a result of information you take in through your visual, auditory and kinaesthetic systems. So modalities are categorized into these three systems.

REPRESENTATIONAL SYSTEM HAS SPECIFIC DISTINCTIONS WITHIN IT THAT BECOME "THE DIFFERENCE THAT MAKES THE DIFFERENCE"

Submodality?

Submodalities are fine distinctions or subsets of modalities. As we mentioned modalities are categorized into these systems visual, auditory, and kinaesthetic. In fact, submodalities add more information to our inner images, sounds, and senses. For instance, you can describe an inner image with colors, size, sharpness, distance, etc. These features are called submodalities. Here are some common submodalities:

**Visual Submodalities:**

- Black and White Or Color
- Near or Far
- Bright or Dim
- Location
- Associated or Dissociated
- Focused or Defocused
- Framed or Unbounded
- Monie or Still
- If A Movie; Fast/Normal/Slow
- 3D or 2D

**Auditory Submodalities:**

- Loud or Soft
- Near or Far
- Internal or External
- Mono or Stereo
- Fast or Slow
- High or Low Pitch
- Verbal or Tonal
- Rhythm

Kinaesthetic Submodalities:

- Breathing rate
- Pulse rate
- Pressure
- movement
- Weight
- Intensity, etc

Olfactory/ Gustatory Submodalities:

- Sweet
- Sour
- Aroma
- Fragrance/Pungence
- Essence
- Salt/Bitter..etc

Submodalities are key components to many of the NLP change techniques. As mentioned earlier submodalities, by themselves or as part of other techniques, have been used to assist people to stop smoking, eat more of certain foods and less of others, address compulsion issues, change beliefs and values, enhance motivation, move from stress to relaxation, address phobias, etc.

SUB-MODALITIES PLAY A GREAT ROLE WHILE CODING THE INFORMATION INTO THE BRAIN!

## FEAR OF DOG

### SUB-MODALITIES

| VISUAL | AUDITORY | KINESTHETIC |
| --- | --- | --- |
| BIG DOG WITH SHARP TEETH | BARKING LOUDLY | MY PULSE RATE & HEART RATE GO FAST |
| SO CLOSE DOG IS | BARKING SO RUDELY | FEELING FEAR |
| DOG IS SO BRIGHT | EARS WERE AFFECTED | DOG IS BITING |
| DANGER COLOUR | SOMEONE IS TELLING ME – DON'T GO NEAR | FEELING SWEATY |
| | | NOT ABLE TO RUN |

## LOVING DOG

## SUB-MODALITIES

### VISUAL

DOGS ARE CUTE
DOG'S COLOUR IS BRIGHT
WAGGING TAIL
DOG IS SMILING

### AUDITORY

DOG TALKING
SOUND IS SO CUTE
DOG IS TELLING ME TO
COME AND HUG

### KINESTHETIC

HUGGING THE DOG
PULSE RATE &
HEART RATE GOES SO MILD
FEELING LOVED
FEELING AWESOME & SAFE
FEELING LIGHT

CHAPTER SIX

# Meta Model

The meta-model in NLP or neuro-linguistic programming (or meta-model of therapy) is a set of questions designed to specify information, and challenge and expand the limits of a person's model of the world.

It responds to the distortions, generalizations, and deletions in the speaker's language. The meta-model forms the basis of Neuro-linguistic programming as developed by then assistant professors of linguistics, John Grinder and Richard Bandler. Grinder and Bandler "explained how people create faulty mental maps of reality, failing to test their linguistic/cognitive models against the experience of their senses."

The meta-model draws on transformational grammar and general semantics, the idea that language is a translation of mental states into words, and that in this translation, there is an unconscious process of deletion (not everything thought is said), distortion (assumptions and structural inaccuracies) and generalization (a shift towards absolute statements). Likewise in hearing, not everything said is acknowledged as heard.

Following are EXAMPLES of HOW to use your language to recover lost sensory experiences from the speaker:

**Deletion:**

**1. Vague Subject: Who/What Exactly?**

•They are not sincere

•Some people dislike me

•Certain things are bothering me

**2. Vague Actions:**

Intervention 1: How exactly...

Intervention 2: What exactly...

Intervention 3: What needs to happen for you to know that...

•Mr.X is not performing

•You are not supporting me

•He does not understand me
•You don't love/like me

**3. Comparison: compared to what?/who?**

•Your product is too costly
•This work is too tough

**4. Opinion as a fact: according to whom?**

•Money spoils our character
•Health is not in our control

**Distortion:**

**1. Mind Reading: how exactly do you know that?**

•You look upset
•He was angry
•She is depressed

**2. Interpretations: How does 'X' mean 'Y'?**

•He doesn't look at me, he dislikes me
•Today also you came late, you don't respect me
•It's raining heavily, It's a bad day

**Generalization:**

**1. Universals: all, never, always, everyone, nobody**

•All political leaders are dishonest
•You always irritate me
•Everyone likes honesty

**2. Stoppers: what stops you? Or what would happen if you did it?**

Use of Can't
•I can't do this work
•I can't learn this language
•I can't apply this skill

**3. Drivers: what forces you? What would happen if you didn't?**

Use have to, must, should, ought to
•They are accompanied by a feeling of tension
•I have to finish the job by evening
•I have to go to the office daily
•You must save money regularly

**Quiz**

**1.No body loves me**

Nobody?

**2. Money is very bad**

Who told you?

**3. You are looking depressed/worried**
How do you know that I am depressed?
**4. I can't do this work**
What stops you?
**5. All political leaders are corrupted.**
All?
**6. Today you came late, you don't love me/respect**
How coming late means that I don't love you, dear/sir?
**7. Money spoils our character/relation**
According to whom?
**8. This work is tough/difficult**
What exactly is tough in this work?
**9. This product is costly**
Compared to what?
**10. He is not supporting me/ love me**
How exactly do you want him to support you or love you?
**11. He doesn't love me**
How exactly do you want him to love you?
**12. Those are not good people**
Who exactly?

**Case Studies**

**Case1:**
If you ask a student about his college/school.
He may say it's not good.
He deleted good things from his memory.
**Case2:**
If a student says my parents don't love me or care about me.
I am not happy.
He deleted all the good things/He remembered the situation when he got a low score/his parents' reactions.
**Case3:**
Husband is irritated by his wife's words/ or in an irritation state(wife is an anchor to this emotion)
What husband really needs Attention, Love
He may be hungry
Solution: She may respond this way "Tell me, sweetheart!! ? with a smile.
**Case4:**
One girl feels insecurity

Because their classmates are teasing her, commenting on her, etc.

Solution: She changes her body language and smile on her face and reframing the words below

They don't have other work.

I may have to show my strengths.

Even if some heroes/Heroine come here

they will comment on them as well. It is their nature

**Case5:**

Raju prepared his presentation and was ready to go to the meeting.

His car is not working. He changed his words like this

At least I have a car others don't have.

I can book Ola, Uber may inform the office that I will come late.

He presented well.

**Case6:**

I am dancing. 3 people's points of view. 1$^{st}$ person says - He doesn't have any work so he is dancing now.2$^{nd}$ person says- Nice dance 3$^{rd}$ person says- He is a good dancer

**Case7:**

Some people are always happy, successful, confident, afraid, panicked, etc.

They are deleting the happy moments/sad moments and focusing on other things.

**Homework**

If you forgot your keys or other things

How you speak with yourself or others (linguistic)

If you create negativity, try to change it to positive and focus on what you can do.

Take any 3 situations in your daily routine and apply this method and see the outcomes.

CHAPTER SEVEN

# Break or Build a Habit

**Break a habit:**

- •Reduce the time or quantity of bad habit
- •Like chocolates 1st week -8 chocolates
- •2nd- 6 chocolates...
- •5th week- 1

**Build a Habit:**

•Start doing the task for 5 Minutes/day for a week and
•then 10min/day for next week
•then.......30min next week.....
**Example:** Reading a book, meditation..etc

CHAPTER EIGHT

# Eye Accessing Cues

According to neurological research, eye movement both laterally and vertically seems to be associated with activating different parts of the brain. In the neurological literature, these movements are called lateral eye movements (LEM) and in NLP we call them eye-accessing cues because they give us insights into how people are accessing information.

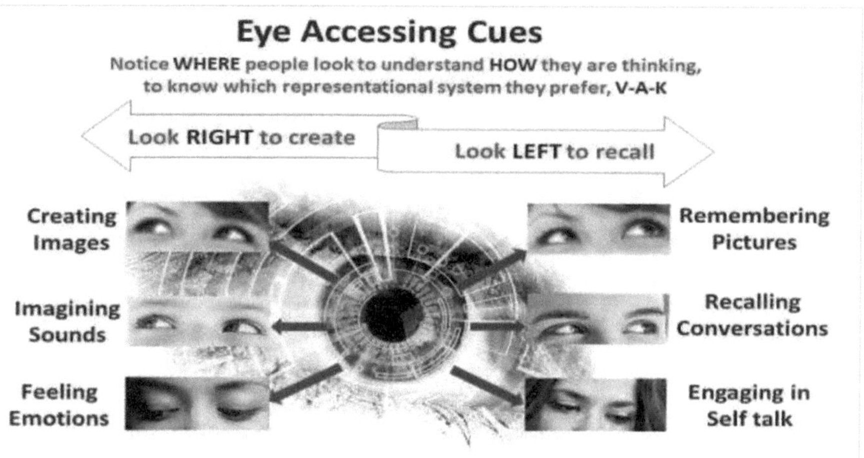

**IMAGINED VISUAL**

**Up and to the right**

- creating a picture of something never seen
- creative visualization
- possibly lying or making up a visual

**VISUAL MEMORY**

**Up and to the left**

- remembering a picture or image
- recalling a scene witnessed

**IMAGINED AUDITORY**

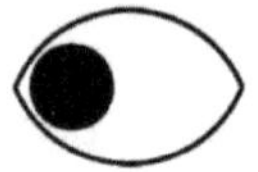

**To the right**

- imagine one sound morphing into another
- making up a tune
- writing a poem
- possibly lying or making up words

**AUDITORY MEMORY**

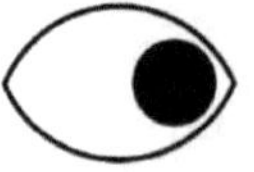

**To the left**

- remembering a sound
- recalling a tune previously heard
- remembering a poem

**FEELINGS**

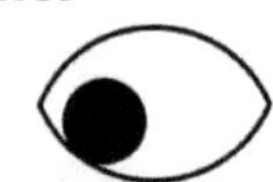

**Down and to the right**

- recalling an emotion
- imagining an emotion
- remembering a physical feeling
- imagining a physical feeling

**INTERNAL SELF TALK**

**Down and to the left**

- listening to the voice inside
- talking to oneself

To get an idea of how your eyes move, consider the following questions. For each question, as you think of the answer, notice the direction(s) your eyes move (up down, or to the side), or if your eyes do not seem to move notice if you have a sense that you are looking in a certain direction (even if only for a fraction of a second).

What is the color of your front door?
What will you look like in 15 years?
What does your favorite music sound like?
What would your voice sound like if you had marbles in your mouth?
When you talk to yourself, what type of voice do you use?
What does it feel like to be in a nice warm bath?

Did you notice your eyes had a tendency to look up for the first two questions, to the side for the next two questions, and down for the last two questions? In general, if you are making a picture in your mind your eyes will tend to go up to the left or the right, for sounds laterally to the left or right, and down to the left or right for feelings or when you talk to yourself.

More specifically, if you are right-handed, you may have noticed the following (for people who are left-handed, interchange left and right in the following text):

**Question 1** - eyes up and to your left. This is a question about something you have seen before and hence you remembered it -- visual remembered (VR).

**Question 2** - eyes up and to your right. This is a question about something that I assume you have not seen before and hence you constructed this picture - visual constructed (VC).

**Question 3** - eyes on the horizontal plane to your left. This is a question about something you have heard before - auditory remembered (AR).

**Question 4** - eyes on the horizontal plane to your right. This is a question about something you have not heard before - auditory construction (AC).

**Question 5** - eyes down and to the left. This is a question about your self-talk - auditory digital (Ad).

**Question 6** - eyes down and to the right. This is a question about your feelings- kinesthetic (K).

CHAPTER NINE

# Outcome

Coach yourself and others to achieve big goals.

A definite question in NLP: *' What do you want?*

In NLP outcomes are different from targets/goals/objectives,because,they(outcomes)meet certain conditions

that makes them realistic/motivating/achievable.

Tasks differ from outcomes. Outcomes; what you want, task; what you do to get what you want.

Don't do tasks until you set your outcomes.

Problem?

The gap between what you have and what you want.

**Proactive**

Enter Caption

•Set an outcome and be clear about your desired state, plan to make the journey from one to the other, take ownership of the problem, and start to move towards a solution. Problems can't be solved unless you have an outcome.

•Present State to Desired State( with resource)

•Journey from Present State(Ps) to Desire State(Ds)

Outcome thinking questions: Developing outcome thinking!

•1. What am I moving towards? (DS or Outcome)

•2. By When will I get there? (The deadline)

•3. Why am I moving? (Values that Guide you)

•4. How will I get there? (The strategy for the journey)

•5. What if something goes wrong? (Risk Management)

CHAPTER TEN

# 9 Step Formula For Guaranteed Success

**Structure Your Outcomes**

•The well-formed conditions:

**1. Positive:**

What you want

•Your outcome should be positive

•? *No- not poor, not angry, not struck, not fat, not lazy* _Mind can't accept them_

**2. Evidence:**

How will you know you are succeeding/have succeeded?

Eg .1. Milestones

•Going to Goa

Eg.2. Weight loss

•10kg- 1 month

•Weekly -2.5 kg

•350gm- per day

•Daily 10 min exercise

**3. Specifics:**

when/where/with whom

•Object,date/time

•?Lot,big success,loose more weight

**4. Resources**

•a.objects b. People c. Role models d. Personal qualities e. Money

i. Internal resources

•a.Time b.interest c.Knowledge and. d.Skills

ii. External

• a.Money b.Support c.Hardware(laptop,books)

Ex:

•Children are very interested in games and not interested in studies.

Week resources in studies:

•Lazy, stubborn, no skill, dull

Power resources in games like cricket

•Active, Energetic, skills, enthusiasm, money, time

**5. Control:**

Can you start/maintain the outcome (direct control); if others; who will help you, and how you will motivate them?

• Self-start,

•self manage,

• self-control

**6. Ecology:** Wider Consequences

•What is the price; time and effort?

•Who else is affected? How do they feel? What significance is at stake?

•Think of the Present State (What is good about it? What do you want to keep: losing means pain)

**7. Identity:**

Is this outcome consistent with WHO you are?

•You got a job in a remote location will you go there without your family

•Missing, busy, no family time

**8. Chunk Down:** Chunk down if the outcome is large.

•Eg. Writing a book

•1 month

•1 week

•Daily

**9. Action Plan:** What to do Next?

•Act now

CHAPTER ELEVEN

# Identify Your Preferred Thinking Pattern: Questionnaire

•This questionnaire is in no way a definitive analysis but is merely to raise your awareness of how you think. Your thinking patterns may vary from one situation to another.

•The aim of this exercise is to help you identify any preferences you have in your thinking pattern.

•You may tick as many senses as are true for you for any question. You may, for example, have one sense ticked for one question and five for another question. Work through each question and be aware of what comes to mind the moment you see it.

**Questionnaire:**

**1. Chocolate Bar**

•a. An image or picture

•b. A sound

•c. A feeling or an emotion

•d. A taste

•e. A smell

**2. Your best friend**

•a. An image or picture

•b. A sound

•c. A feeling or an emotion

•d. A taste

•e. A smell

**3. The way you would most like to spend your time**

•a. An image or picture.

•b. A sound.

•c. A feeling or an emotion

•d. A taste

•e. A smell.

**4. What you did do last Sunday.**

•a. An image or picture

•b. A sound.

•A feeling or an emotion

•d. A taste

•e. A smell.

**5. Any function or party where you enjoyed most**

a. An image or picture.

•b. A sound.

•c. A feeling or an emotion

•d. A taste

•e. A smell.

**6. Your favorite restaurant**
•a. An image or picture
•b. A sound.
•A feeling or an emotion
•d. A taste
•e. A smell.
**7. Something from your childhood**
a. An image or picture.
•b. A sound.
•c. A feeling or an emotion
•d. A taste
•e. A smell.
**8. Something from work**
•a. An image or picture
•b. A sound.
•A feeling or an emotion
•d. A taste
•e. A smell.
**9. Where you may be tomorrow?**
a. An image or picture.
•b. A sound.
•c. A feeling or an emotion
•d. A taste
•e. A smell.
**10. Something you find difficult to do**
•a. An image or picture
•b. A sound.
•A feeling or an emotion
•d. A taste
•e. A smell.
**11. Something you find rewarding**
a. An image or picture.
•b. A sound.
•c. A feeling or an emotion
•d. A taste
•e. A smell.
**12. Something you find amusing**
a. An image or picture

•b. A sound.

•A feeling or an emotion

•d. A taste

•e. A smell.

**13. A goal that you have fixed for the future.**

a. An image or picture.

•b. A sound.

•c. A feeling or an emotion

•d. A taste

•e. A smell.

**14. Your expectations for the rest of this week**

a. An image or picture

•b. A sound.

•A feeling or an emotion

•d. A taste

•e. A smell.

**15. What are you doing at this moment?**

•a. An image or picture.

•b. A sound.

•c. A feeling or an emotion

•d. A taste

•e. A smell.

CHAPTER TWELVE

# Fast Phobia Cure or Double Dissociation Technique

Rapport position mirroring the physiology mirroring the tonality
Clients need to be in rapport with you.
Phobia is irrational fear-run away
Normal fear-not feel good about it.
You can do this technique with your eyes open or with your eyes closed
I know that it works very well with the eyes closed
Choice of the client's eyes open/eyes closed.

**Eyes closed:**

- Imagine that you and I are both entering a movie theatre and in the movie theatre there's nobody there. The lights are on and there is nothing on the screen.
- And you choose a place to sit. I came with you. You choose a place to sit and you sit in that place and I sit next to you now as magic I pull you out of your body and both of us walk out of the movie theatre.
- We climb up the stairs and go to the projection room.so now we are going to the projection and we enter the projection room.
- You see there's a projector there's a window for that projector from where it projects movies and then there are many movie reels in that projection room and they are all about your life.
- Now you go near the projector and you look through the window and you see the entire movie theatre.
- And you can see yourself sitting in the movie theater. (Double dissociation helps in separating fear)
- Looking at the screen at the moment there is nothing being played on the screen. The screen is blank. Remember you are here in the projection room looking at yourself looking at the screen.
- Now you look around the projector room and you see these reels which are related to your life.
- Right and one such reel you pull out and it's called your phobia and you put that reel on the projector but don't play it yet till I tell you.
- When you play this movie about your phobia you will look at yourself on the movie screen, okay and you are going to play this movie in black and white remember you are in the projector room.
- (Double dissociation)Play the movie in black & white
- So when I say go you will start playing the phobia movie in black and white once you are done then once you have played it from start to end give me a thumbs up and I will.
- Go
- Oh good, Now the screen is all blanked out and now you will be coming with me. We will walk out of the projection room.
- Walk down the steps and again enter the movie theatre now this time you will continue walking towards the movie screen remember there is nothing being played on the screen yet.

- As you walk towards the screen you can see yourself sitting in the movie theatre and you will be going alone towards the screen and finally, you will enter the movie screen.
- Which means you are now a part of that screen.
- As of now, nothing is being played but now when I tell you. You will be running the same phobia movie with you being a part of it in the reverse order, okay
- And this time you will be running it with full color, happiness, music, and balloons like a carnival. the same movie.
- (Process of association)Movies played backward, full colors, happiness, music, and celebrations.
- You are still there on the screen now, this time again you are going to be playing this movie the same way backward in full color but this time you will be playing it twice the speed.
- Go
- Cool
- Again the screen blanked out again to do the same thing at thrice speeds.
- Go
- The screen blanked out again 4 times the speed
- Go
- Cool
- One last time again you play this movie backward in full color as you played it earlier this time 5 times the speed.
- Right
- Now the screen is again blanked out and you now are walking out off the screen and then you will walk towards the place where you are sitting and sit where you are sitting and once you are done with that you'll open your eyes and come back in now.
- Cool
- How are you feeling now?

If you see it again how would things be different/?

CHAPTER THIRTEEN

# Power Pose Technique

**POWER POSE TECHNIQUE :FOCUS + PHYSIOLOGY + POSITIVE WORDS**

**Procedure:**
**Step 1:** Relax your whole body
**Step 2:** Take a few deep breaths
Inhale In

Hold for sometime

Exhale Out - Do it 3 times

**Step 3:** Imagine a Happy moment in your life or Visualise a positive moment that you want to achieve

**Step 4:** Place the hands on the waist & Raise the chest (like a Superman/ woman)

**Step 5:** Say it mentally "I am strong", "I am happy", "I am powerful", "I was born to succeed"

**Step 6:** Relax and slowly open your eyes.

CHAPTER FOURTEEN

# Anchoring Technique

**Procedure:**

**Step 1:** Close your eyes and Relax your whole body

**Step 2:** Take a deep and steady breath in, hold it for some time and breathe out slowly. Do it 3 times

**Step 3:** Now Imagine the happiest moment in your life (Only one moment).

**Eg:** Childhood memories

Met your bestie after a long time

A high score in $10^{th}$ grade

Spent the best time with friends at the beach

Achieved your first dream job

**Step 4:** Visualise that happy moment increased by 10 times, 100 times, 500 times, 1000 times.....NOW Trigger an anchor.

(Hold the anchor (Eg: the Left-hand thumb) for a few seconds and Release))

**Step 5:** Repeat step 3 and 4 two more times

**Step 6:** Relax and slowly open your eyes

**Step 7:** Break concentration. Think about something else for a few sec

**Eg:** Tell your name and phone number in reverse

CHAPTER FIFTEEN

# Fast Track Technique

**Procedure:**

**Step 1:** Close your eyes & Relax your whole body.

**Step 2:** Visualise 'Stress', 'Worries', and 'Anxious' all these negative energies are released in the form of a RED colour race.

From each and every part of your body

Through your legs

Through your waist

Through your abdomen

Through your hands etc.,

Visualise that each part is free from negative energies.

Start visualising from the lower part of the body...The red colour race is released from the left leg

And then the right leg, next left hip, right hip, waist, left hand, right hand, lower back, middle back, upper back, stomach, heart, back of the neck etc.,

**Step 3:** Now Visualise the universe is turning these red colour races into GREEN colour races (positive energies, positive feelings)

These green colour races flow through the nostrils while inhaling and it is spreading to each and every part of the body.

While exhaling, Red colour races are going out.

While inhaling, Green colour races are coming in.

**Step 4:** Repeat 2 & 3 again

**Step 5:** Relax yourself.

**HABITS THAT MAKE ANXIETY WORSE**

- Eating too much chocolate
- Not drinking enough water
- Staying up late
- Checking your phone every minute
- Not moving your body enough(exercise)
- Eating processed food/skipping meals
- Drinking excessively
- Spending all day inside

CHAPTER SIXTEEN

# A New Behaviour Generator

**Procedure:**
**Step 1:** Identify a behavior
**Ex:** A Motivational Speaker
A Professor
A Jovial Person
**Step 2:** Identify a person( a role model)
**Ex:** Sudha Murthy
Deepak Chopra

Gaur Gopal Das

**Step 3:** Follow and Observe that person (all the time)

**Practice Time:**

**Step 4:** Now close your eyes and start visualizing

How does the person behave?

How does he/she motivate?

What are his/her body language & Facial expression?

How is her/his tone?

**Step 5:** Now visualize you are in that person's place. You are imitating the same behavior, the same energy, the same body language & facial expressions & the same tone & voice.

**Step 6:** Relax and slowly open your eyes.

**Step 7:** Repeat step 4, 5 & 6 for few days.

CHAPTER SEVENTEEN

# NLP Circle of Excellence

**Procedure:**

Everyone! Please stand up. Now, you are in position A

**Step 1:** Now close your eyes. Take a deep breath in, Hold it for some time and Breathe out slowly. Do it 3 times. Relax. Don't open your eyes.

**Step 2:** Choose the best happy moment in your life.

Eg: It could be childhood days/ college life/Vacations/meeting a bestie, etc.,

**Step 3:** Right now, imagine you are in that happy situation.

At that moment, What do you see?

How do you speak?

How are your heart rate and pulse rate?

How do you walk?

How do others appreciate you?

How do you feel?

How do you smile? etc.

In the form of visual, auditory & kinesthetic, observe it, and feel it in every aspect clearly.

The same happiness you want to attract again.

**Step 4:** Now come to power pose by placing your hands on your waist.

**Step 5:** Imagine there is a circle in front of you. That is position B

Imagine there is a green color liquid in it. It gives you confidence, energy, health, strength, security, etc., The liquid has all the capabilities.

**Step 6:** Now with eyes closed, you are stepping one step forward from position A to position B

**Step 7:** As soon as the liquid touches your feet, your confidence, your strengths, and your energy level increase.

**Step 8:** Now it starts spreading from feet to knees, knees to hips, hips to waist, waist to shoulders, all the way up to the top of the head.

Imagine your happiness increases by double. Observe it, and Feel the changes in your body. You turn into a GREEN color.

Now you gain all the confidence, strength, and energy in your body.

**Step 9:** Now liquid is returning to the circle. Feel it.

**Step 10:** Now Release your hands on your waist. Come Back to position A.

**Step 11:** Again Repeat steps 4 to step 10

**Step 12:** Imagine there is a kerchief with you. You are dropping it in the liquid and collecting some liquid from it.

**Step 13:** keep the kerchief in your pocket. whenever you need it, use it.

**Step 14:** Relax yourself & slowly open your eyes.

CHAPTER EIGHTEEN

# To Overcome Procrastination

Actually What happens?
When we decide to adopt a new habit/pattern/task/ activity /behavior
After 2 to 3 days of doing it, The stress hormone is released by the brain
Trigger (Stress released by the brain)
—> Pattern(Stop doing the new task)

—> Reward(Relaxed mood, Eg: watching FB, Tiktok)
—> As a result, postpone the task

CHAPTER NINETEEN

# Just 5 minutes Rule Technique

**Procedure:**

**Step 1:** Relax your whole body. Close your eyes.

**Step 2:** Now, say it to yourself orally or mentally.

"I am going to do this new task/activity for JUST 5 minutes."

"Only just 5 minutes."

**Step 3:** Repeat it 3 times

**Step 4:** Slowly allow your eyes to open.

Once you change the state. automatically, you can do more than 5 minutes.

CHAPTER TWENTY

# Just 5 seconds Rule Technique

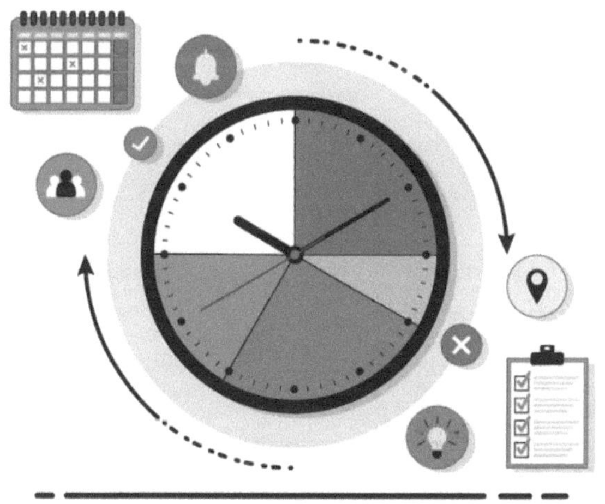

**Procedure:**

Apply this technique, when you feel tense, nervous, lazy, or fear

**Step 1:** Relax your whole body. Close your eyes

**Step 2:** Count mentally 5....4....3....2...1... Go

**Step 3:** Slowly open your eyes.

**Step 4:** Start doing the task without any other thought. :)

CHAPTER TWENTY-ONE

# Disney Creative Strategy

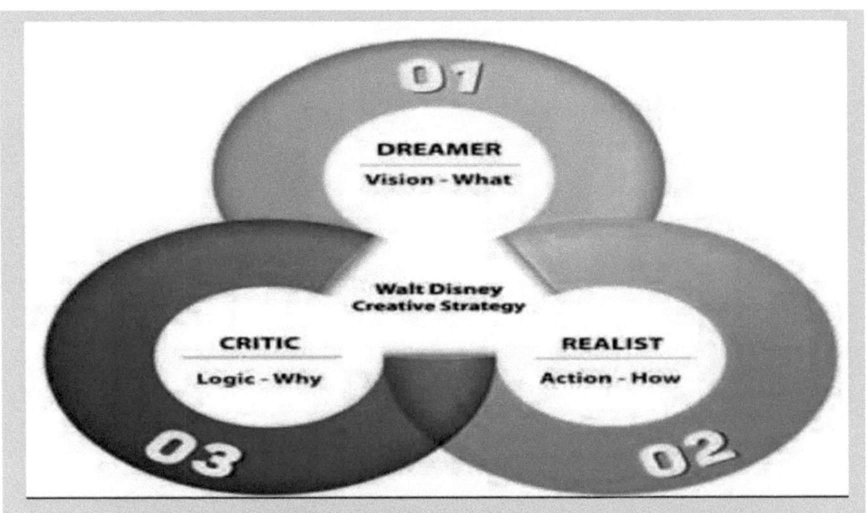


Enter Caption

**Procedure:**

(Apply this technique for a better career, and set goals. To overcome the confused state and negative thinking)

3 people within you

First - Dreamer

Second - Realistic person

Third - Critic person

**Dreamer:** (Stand straight facing forward)

**Step 1:** Close your eyes. Relax your body.

**Step 2:** Imagine you are a dreamer now. Just think only about your dreams/ your wishes/ your desires.

Important note: it doesn't matter whether they are possible or not

**Step 3:** Imagine every aspect of your life, in terms of family, finances, career, relationships, health, professional life, house, lands, etc.,

Remember, there is no limit. Whether it is a small desire or a big desire, it doesn't matter.

You can just think of any dreams/ wishes you want to...

Unlimited wishes

No restrictions! No boundaries for you

**Eg:**

Dream 1: I want to be a great motivational speaker.

Dream 2: I want to be a pilot

Dream 3: I want to be a perfectly healthy

Dream 4: I want to write a book

Dream 5: I want to be a good partner

Dream 6: I want to go on a world tour

Dream 7: I want to earn 5k per month

.

.

.

. Etc.,

Step 4: Relax yourself and open your eyes.

Step 5: Write down every dream in your book.

**Realistic person:** (Stand straight facing the left side)

**Step 1:** Close your eyes and relax your body

**Step 2:** Imagine you are a realistic person. Now Dreamer gave the big list to the realistic person.

**Step 3:** Now the realistic person has to organize them and do a priority list properly. And also has to check which is possible and which is not possible.

A priority list (the most important dream comes first and then second and next... so on)

Dream 1...

Dream 2...

Dream 3...

.

.

.etc.,

**Step 4:** Slowly open your eyes.

**Step 5:** Write down the first dream

**Eg:** Dream 1:

How much time takes to achieve that? Days/weeks/months/years

What skills are needed?

What resources & support are required?

Etc.,

**Important note:** Write it in detail

And then Dream 2:

Dream 3:

Dream 4:

.

.

. So on

Critic person (Stand straight facing right side)

A Critical person is your best friend. He guides you and suggests you

**Step 1:** Relax your body and close your eyes

**Step 2:** Imagine you are a critical person now. The realistic gave the organized list to you

**Step 3:** The critical person has to take one dream at a time and identify its good qualities and its weaknesses.

A priority list:

Dream 1... Good qualities and bad qualities

Dream 2...

Dream 3...

.

.

.etc.,

**Eg:** Dream 1:

*Good qualities: *

Eg: Waking up early

Eating mindfully

Organizing the tasks

Journaling

Reading a book etc.,

Weakness:

Eg: laziness

Late-night sleep
Doing multiple tasks at a time
Watching mobile frequently etc.,
Dream 2:
Dream 3:
.
.
.so on

**Ask yourself these questions:**

Which qualities are not allowing you to achieve your goals?
How to overcome it?
What is stopping you?
What can be done to achieve my goal?

**Step 4:** Slowly open your eyes

**Step 5:** Write it down clearly.

CHAPTER TWENTY-TWO

# Say NO to Distractions - Concentrate Better

**Procedure:**
(To improve concentration)
When you start doing any task/activity
**Eg:** Reading a book
Follow these 3 steps.
**Step 1:** "I won't be distracted by that anymore."
Or "I focus on what I am doing right now."

Write it down on paper.

**Step 2:** Now Set a stopwatch for 5 mins

**Step 3:** Do tally marks, when you distract each time.

When you achieve zero distractions, next do it for 7 mins, and then 10 mins,15 mins... So on.

CHAPTER TWENTY-THREE

# Rapport Building Technique

(mirroring/matching/leading)

Rapport is the establishment of trust and harmony in a relationship.

Rapport indicates that there is some similarity and likeness between you and the other. Without rapport, you will never gain the support and cooperation of other people.

There are a number of levels at which rapport may be established.

1. Personality type.
2. Gender, Religion, Politics, Culture, Ethnicity
3. Values, beliefs, and interests.
4. How you dress.

5. How you position your body.

6. How you talk including the type of words that you use.

In some cases, you may find it easier to establish and maintain rapport with someone who has a similar personality type - that is they share similar meta programs to you.

The same goes for people who share similar religious and political views - and values, beliefs, and interests.

How you dress - your culture and ethnicity all play a part in establishing rapport.

To establish rapport you need to mirror the other person in some way- you need to show them in some way that you are similar - that you are alike.

*Apply this technique, to convince others, to make a friendship *

**Step 1:** Mirroring the person

**Step 2:** Now Find whether the person is a Visual type/Auditory type/ Kinesthetic type.

**Step 3:** If he/she is a Visual type of person,

- They speak fast.
- Their breath is heavy.
- Hand movements above the ears.
- They maintain eye contact.
- They generally talk about visual-related things.
- They like images/videos/Displays/slide presentations.
- They are generally convinced by seeing pictures/views/displays
- If he/she is an auditory type of person,
- They speak selective words only
- Their tone clear
- Their breathing normal
- Hand movements up to ears
- They maintain normal eye contact
- They generally talk about audio-related things
- They like pleasant sounds/music/songs/attractive speech
- They are generally convinced by listening to selective words/ attractive talks/sound related things
- If he/she is a kinesthetic type of person,
- They don't maintain eye contact
- They talk less
- Hand movements are low

- They have Relaxed breathing
- They usually connect with feelings

**Step 4:** Try to match 70% with them. But not 100% and lead them.
**Eg:** matching: hand movements, words

CHAPTER TWENTY-FOUR

# Timeline Technique

(How to delete the negative memories/experiences?)

(How to learn lessons from them and accept them?)

(How to build a bring future?)

**Note:** if you find it difficult to think about the past, turn your eyes to the top left corner with closed eyes.

**Procedure:**

**Step 1:** Stand up. Close your eyes and relax your body.

**Step 2:** Think of a past negative experience( Eg: an insult on a college day). Make sure you only learn a lesson from it. NOW you want to delete that experience.

**Step 3:** Imagine there is a dustbin behind you. Now Take that experience with your left hand. Throw it back and let it BLAST...!?

Now take another bad experience(Eg: feeling Shy) and do the same.

**Step 4:** Repeat step 2 & 3 until you don't have any bad exp.

Think of a bad experience —> Learn lessons from it—> Delete it—> Throw it in the dustbin—> let It BLAST...?

**Step 5:** Now think of good memories/experiences (Eg: playing with besties) on the right side of your body. Place them from the right side to the left side. Now you are filled with good exp on the left side of your body.

**Step 6:** keep continuing step 5 until you feel joyful and energetic.

If you find visualization difficult, turn your eyes to the top right corner

**Step 7:** Visualise you are in 2022 on June $1^{st}$. You have done an awesome job by finishing the NLP course and exam. In July you are practicing all techniques very well and you have started counseling people and teaching the course. Everyone is benefiting from your teachings and they are appreciating you.

*Imagine that happiness NOW. You are so confident and energetic *

**Step 8:** Repeat step 7 (by visualizing the same in August, September,..... January 2023 you are a new person... January 2024....January 2025)

**Step 9:** you are returning on May $25^{th}$, 2022. Relax... Slowly open your eyes.

CHAPTER TWENTY-FIVE

# Self-Improvement Journaling – Method– Reflective Journaling

Journaling for reflection is the simple act of letting your mind wander, and scribbling down whatever thoughts come to mind as you reflect on your day. You can do this in paragraphs or as bullets—capturing as much or as little detail as you like.

Most of the time, we move through our days so quickly that we have little time to absorb and process what happens to us. As we take time to write about different experiences and events, we can start to see larger connections. If it's helpful, you can structure your entries by answering a series of questions:

What happened?

What was its impact on you?

What did you learn?

What are the implications?

Over time, themes will appear and you will learn what you think—and how you feel—about the events of your life.

**Tools needed:** A journal and a pen

CHAPTER TWENTY-SIX

# Swish Technique 1

**Visual Type**
Change submodalities
Erase the picture with a Duster
**Step 1:** Relax your body. Close your eyes
**Step 2:** Recall the image(Scared/Horror) that you want to delete forever.
**Step 3:** Now visualize changing the color of the image (Eg: Green color)

**Step 4:** Now visualize changing the size of the image (Eg: Elephant size/ Moose size) and placing a cherry on their nose.

We changed the horror image to a funny image

**Step 5:** Relax yourself. Slowly open your eyes.

**Note:** Repeat this technique for a few days.

CHAPTER TWENTY-SEVEN

# Swish Technique 2

**Step 1:** Relax your body. Close your eyes

**Step 2:** Recall the old image(Scared/afraid)that you want to delete forever.

**Step 3:** Now visualize the old image fading away.

**Step 4:** Now Visualise creating a new relaxed confident picture with your friend. Both are smiling.

**Step 5:** I am taking that new image. Now I throw this new image like a ball with 2x speed to break the old one.

Swishhhhh.....

**Step 6:** The old image is broken. Again I have taken the new image and thrown at a 3x speed

Swishhhh....

**Step 7:** It's broken into minor pieces.

**Step 8:** Now this time 6x speed.

Swishhhh....

**Step 9:** The old image is no longer anymore.

**Step 10:** Visualise and replace a new energetic relaxed smiling picture. Now it is bright, colorful, and large in front of you.

**Step 11:** Relax and slowly open your eyes.

CHAPTER TWENTY-EIGHT

# Pain Relief Technique

**Overcome Pain Instantly Using NLP**

**Step 1:** First identify the part where you are feeling pain.

**Step 2:** On a scale of 10, give a number to that pain. How intense the pain is.

**Step 3:** visualize yourself holding that pain and you are expanding and compressing it.

**Step 4:** Now put that pain into a television. It has knobs. Whether You increase the brightness or reduce it to black.

**Step 5:** Using your hands, write on the screen. All is well/ I am perfectly healthy/ I am happy/ I am relaxed/ I am calm.

**Step 6:** Using your hands, turn the pain into a small coin like a nail. Now forcefully throw the nail away to the wall.

**Step 7:** Relax yourself

Now Moving to **the Relaxation Technique**

Enter Caption

Step 1: Identify the comfortable part of your body. (Eg: maybe your heart, your eyes...)

Step 2: Visualise that comfortable/soft feeling spreading all over the body. You feel relaxed and light now.

Step 3: Relax yourself. Slowly open your eyes.

CHAPTER TWENTY-NINE

# Dissociation Technique-Anger Management Technique

**Procedure:**

**Step 1:** Everyone! Sit comfortably. Close your eyes. Relax your body.

**Step 2:** Take a deep breath in, hold it for some time, and breathe out slowly. Do it 3 times.

**Step 3:** Relax yourself and please follow the instructions.

**Step 4:** visualize you are sitting on a sofa/couch in front of you there is a big screen tv.

**Step 5:** Visualise on that screen, you see the person who irritates you or The person you don't like or you are angry about him/her.

**Step 6:** Imagine there is a bucket full of white paint in it. Now you pour all the paint on him/her from the top of your head. Now he/she is in white color. Imagine they are becoming smaller and smaller to the size of moose and you hear a helpless voice, asking for help. They say please help me! Please help me!

**Step 7:** Imagine now taking him/her into your hands and say I leave you and I forgive you. And leave them on the ground.

**Step 8:** Relax yourself

**Step 9:** Repeat steps 6, 7 & 8 with 2 buckets, and the third time 3 buckets of paint.

**Step 10:** Relax and slowly open your eyes.

CHAPTER THIRTY

# Neurological Alignment

(Different Mind Levels)

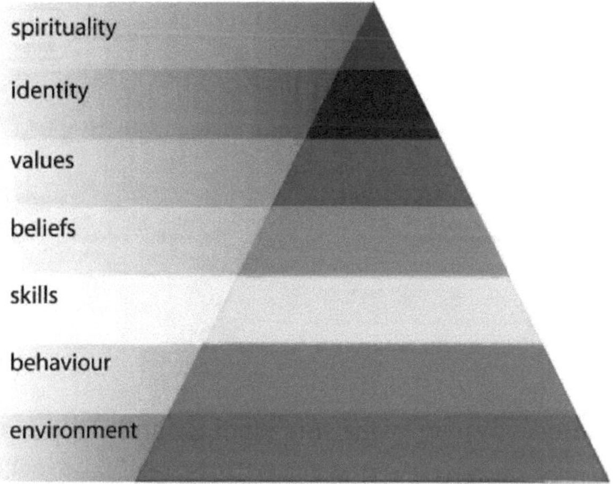


The mind relates to the world around it on different levels, according to NLP. If you want to operate effectively in a certain role, all the levels have to be in alignment.

**For example,**

You want to assume the role of a yoga teacher. Being a yoga teacher will mean you will have to work in a certain environment, a studio or maybe a gym for example.

Also, you will have to behave like a yoga teacher: appropriate body language, voice, and clothes. Not everyone can become a yoga teacher, though.

You need to have certain abilities, for example, the capability of gaining yoga teaching qualifications and being able to explain and demonstrate the poses.

To decide to become a yoga teacher in the first place, you'll possess certain values and beliefs. You'll believe that imparting your knowledge is important and you'll value your profession.

You'll also identify yourself as a yoga teacher and others will do so as well. At a deeper level, you'll see teaching and practicing yoga as part of your life's mission.

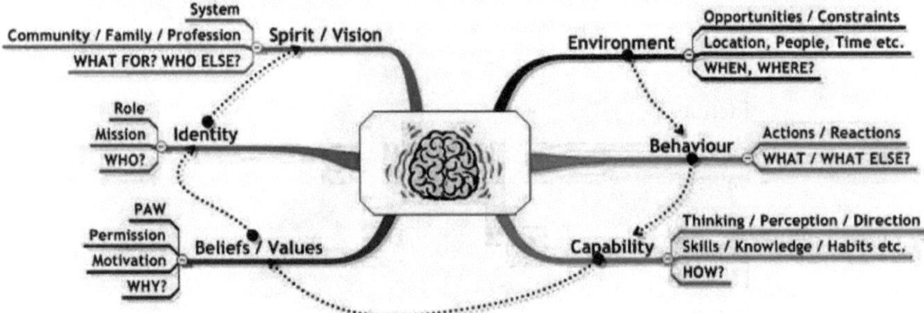


**Environment** — Where: your surroundings and the people you engage with.

**Behaviour** — What: external behaviors, what other people notice

**Capability & Skills** — How: physical, mental and emotional abilities

**Beliefs & Values** — Why: believing whether something is impossible/possible, motivation, and also what is important to you.

**Identity** —Who: Where do you get your self-esteem from and what do you identify with?

**Spiritual** — What for/Who else: your vision for your life and how you relate to the larger system (family, community, global systems).

CHAPTER THIRTY-ONE

# Achieving Your Goals

(Why You Need to Reward Yourself)

When you're trying to make a lifestyle change for weight loss or even for overall health, it's difficult to keep going even when you have a powerful why or reason.

But, on a day-to-day basis when you're in the thick of it all, rewarding yourself in simple ways for small accomplishments can go a long way.

Why? It's all about dopamine. Dopamine spikes in your brain when something important is about to happen and gives you a surge of pleasure as you accomplish the task. This in turn increases motivation and productivity.

Use this piece of science to your advantage by giving yourself small rewards along the way to a bigger goal.

Your brain latches on to the physical evidence that your workout or healthy eating habits are worth it, and increases your chances of making the routine a habit.

**Reward technique**

**Examples of small rewards:**

1. Take yourself out to breakfast
2. Read a book you enjoy for 15–30 minutes
3. Make a dessert
4. Buy yourself a new book
5. Watch one or two episodes of your favorite show
6. Turn off any and all screens for an hour and enjoy the peace
7. Host a game night with friends
8. Buy a new water bottle
9. Watch the sunrise or sunset

Not all of these will appeal to you, and that's where you get to be creative. Reward yourself with the things that motivate and appeal to you. This will ensure that even the small rewards are enough to get you off the couch and moving.

CHAPTER THIRTY-TWO

# Parenting-Habit of book reading for child

1. Read to your child Early and Often
2. Be a Good Role Model
3. Set Challenges and Rewards
4. Set a Daily Reading Time
5. Read what Interests the child
6. Gift them Books
7. Surround your child with Books

CHAPTER THIRTY-THREE

# NLP Reframing

NLP reframing is one of the most fundamental methods of getting change or changing perspective about almost anything.

NLP reframing techniques can be used to change behavior, focus on real problems, or identify hidden resources.

Types of NLP reframing techniques.

1. Context reframing:

In simple words, When a person deletes the context while communicating, that puts behavior in context.

You can identify these statements as “I am too” or “that person is too.”

For Example.

“I am too obsessed with small details.”

“XYZ is too shy to speak.”

Well, I can not be too obsessed with small details in all contexts, right?

Let's see the process of the NLP context reframing technique.

**Step 1**- Identify a resourceful state.

You can choose any behavior, state, event, belief, or some other aspect of yourself that can be useful for context reframing.

You can choose the event where you felt most confident about yourself or when you felt you have all the resources you need.

**Step 2**- Ask Context questions.

Ask yourself where this aspect would be useful.

Imagine the event where this behavior or the expressions will serve you most positively.

**Step 3** – Imagine yourself expressing this aspect in the most appropriate context.

You can take a deep breath and think of the future event to use this aspect positively and to your advantage.

**Step 4** – Select the variety of context for this aspect

You can select various contexts for this aspect; you can try and apply each of them to this aspect.

You can later see which one can be most useful to you in the future.

For example, Can you use the negotiation frame for the relationship aspect? What will be good and bad?

You can do this in as much context as you can think of.

**Step 5** – Test

Ask yourself the following questions after changing the context.

Are you more flexible with choices now?

Are you more creative at problem-solving now?

Can you think of an event where you can use this in your day-to-day use?

NLP Content Reframing

The NLP content reframing technique can be useful where we see our behavior at the event as a mistake or a disadvantage.

NLP Content reframing is used when we do not like our response to the event or our behavior in general.

The NLP content reframing is useful when we want to change our perception of anything that could be judged as negative or positive.

Here is the brief NLP Content reframing technique process we can use.

**Step 1** – Select the behavior to work on

Select the pattern of behavior to work on, and try to select the pattern which occurs regularly.

**Step 2** – Identify the parts involved.

Note the part that is involved in this behavior. Imagine what part of you produces this behavior from you.

Give a name to that part.

**Step 3** – Find positive intention.

Every behavior has a positive intention; find your positive intention of yours for this type of behavior.

**Step 4** – Identify the frame.

What frame is around the intention and behavior?

To identify the frame, observe the presuppositions and generalizations you have while thinking of this behavior or the event.

**Step 5** – Defame the part.

You can ask yourself what else this could mean to me.

Here expand your perspective of yours this event or behavior.

You can also ask what this behavior and intention mean to you, and see the modalities and submodalities involved.

**Step 6** – Reframe the behavior and the intention.

Find the way that enables you to revert to this part, behavior, or intent positively. The reaction can be slight also.

**Step 7** – Reframe the usefulness in terms of the event.

Ask yourself how this behavior can actually be helpful in some other events.

The behavior may need to take a different form or may cease to exist.

Connect with this, how you can feel good about this part in another situation?

You can also find the underlying motivation for this behavior and can learn to use this motivation in other events.

**Step 8** – Accept and integrate the reframe

Allow yourself to use this new reframe for other events or part in another situation.

As it highlights the positive aspect, you may find ways to connect with other situations.

**Step 9**- Test

At last, test the reframe, and think about how you feel now when you think of this behavior or event.

You must be feeling the change in your perspective, self-esteem, and less conflict with the event. If not, do the NLP content reframing technique one more time.

What would be better? If you find ways to utilize those underlying motivations to your advantage for other events.

NLP Context reframing and NLP Content reframing process stated above can be used in moderation in almost any aspect, part, event, and behavior.

**NLP Reframing Questions**

NLP reframing with language allows everyone to see the words differently, which changes the meaning. Once the meaning is changed, our behavior and response to the event also change.

NLP reframing question for NLP context reframing.

In what context will this behavior be helpful?

In what context this behavior be appropriate?

In any context, does this behavior potentially serve me better?

In what way could this behavior be more resourceful?

Have this behavior helped me in the past?

NLP reframing question for NLP content reframing.

What is the positive intention of this event or behavior?

What else could this behavior really mean?

What is the purpose that they do this? Or I do this?

What can be useful about this experience?

Is there any other way I could interpret the meaning of the statement or mistake?

What could I learn from this event?

What I did do well?

These are the sample questions you can use along with the process mentioned above.

Now let's see some of the NLP reframing examples.

NLP reframing examples

I am sharing these NLP reframing examples from my practice and some of the books I have read on the same topic.

NLP reframing examples for NLP context reframing.

Put the behavior in context, and what was once a disadvantage becomes the resource.

**For Example.**

"I am too stubborn."

Reframe -"Well, you must be getting your point heard in those difficult meetings, or you must be good at negotiations."

"I am not ruthless enough."

Reframe '"You must be a very good father because of it."

"I am too bossy."

Reframe – "You must be best at driving meetings."

NLP reframing examples for NLP content reframing.

For content reframing, take a look at the bigger picture and move your focus to other available resources.

**For Example.**

"I feel bad when no one likes my posts on Facebook."

Reframe – " Do you think that allows you to think of better content, or you may need to engage more with them?"

" I had to buy a small car."

Reframe – " Isn't it great, and you will be able to save a great deal on fuel?"

CHAPTER THIRTY-FOUR

# Meta Programs

Meta programs are deletion filters. They cause us to put our attention in certain places and not in others, resulting in habitual patterns of thinking, decision-making, and behavior.

They work at a deep unconscious level, having a strong influence on our behavior, motivation, and personality.

They form a part of the unconscious communication message.

1. Towards/Away from (Motivation direction)

2. Frame of Reference(Internal-External)
3. Matcher-Mismatcher
4. Possibility vs Necessity
5. Option or Procedure
6.Prefrence(Primary Interest)

CHAPTER THIRTY-FIVE

# Money NLP

Money NLP has 5 power elements

1. Competency area with skill
2. Communication skills
3. Personality development
4. Belief transformation
5. Value management

- Money is created twice
- Your money listens, sees, and feels you, so behave with respect!
- Power of a positive environment
- Following the rich, not their family members' environment is more important than heredity.
- Belief transformation through NLP
- “Fear of scarcity” will make it true for you!
- Law of increasing whatever we praisc, that grows!
- Law of supply everything is available. abundance is the law of nature.

Money therapy starts here! ( keep something in your hand which is dynamic in nature, can be kept for the future, and feel good when you have it )

- Be specific, how much do you want?
- The money you are seeking is seeking you in return.
- rich people create a rich vibration!
- Positive virtual identity based on money
- Value management through NLP
- The big the purpose the big the money
- Love people, use money treat money as a servant, people as Guru.

CHAPTER THIRTY-SIX

# Association Technique

**Procedure:**

**Step 1:** Close your eyes and Relax your whole body

**Step 2:** Take a deep and steady breath in, hold it for some time and breathe out slowly. Do it 3 times

**Step 3:** Now Imagine the happiest moment in your life (Only one moment).

**Eg:** Childhood memories

Met your bestie after a long time

A high score in 10th grade

Spent the best time with friends at the beach

Achieved your first dream job

**Step 4:** Visualise that happy moment increased by 10 times, 100 times, 500 times, and 1000 times.

**Step 5:** Repeat step 3 and 4 two more times

**Step 6:** Relax and slowly open your eyes.

CHAPTER THIRTY-SEVEN

# Parenting-How to stop child from getting bored

An important aspect of children's life you know when a kid comes and tells you papa or mama I'm getting bored so what parents immediately think is it is our duty to make them enjoy getting them engaged. You know we can't engage them 24x7.

And it is very important for your parents to note that letting them feel bored you know getting bored is a very critical aspect and it is an important aspect when we feel bored our creative thinking our creativity comes up so students or kids will start thinking what to do to get this boredom away from them.

And this is an important aspect all parents need to remember whenever their kid comes and tells you papa I am getting bored mama I'm getting bored so you don't give them mobile phones and tell them now play now it is your duty so don't think that it is your duty to engage them 24x7 once they reach four years or 5 years it is their duty to check what they can explore and getting bored is a first step to get creative.

So if you want to make your kids creative, let them feel bored, and let them have their own trying they will try everything they will try music, sports, and everything, and then they will come up with creative aspects so remember dear parents it is not your duty to make them feel engaged 24x7.

I see my sister's kid when he comes and feels that he is bored. Sometimes you know she starts engaging with him with his books but otherwise, he has to find his own way of creative learning so getting bored is quite common. We cannot engage with them 24x7.

And all your life it is their duty to check what they can explore and they will find their own means to you know getting out of that bore and that is how the creativity comes.

So dear parents let them feel bored, let them find their own creative methods to come out of that boredom and that's how they generate a hobby and that hobby becomes a passion and they can do great things in their life right.

CHAPTER THIRTY-EIGHT

# Happiness Chemicals & How to Hack Them

YOUR CURRENT STATE OF HAPPINESS IS DETERMINED BY THE LEVELS OF FOUR CHEMICALS IN YOUR BRAIN.

Just remember "DOSE" – Dopamine, Oxytocin, Serotonin, and Endorphins. Here is a list of hacks to get more of those chemicals.

DOPAMINE

The Reward Hormone

Dopamine is known as "The reward Hormone" It's very important for focus and concentration (and sleep!). It's released after your brain achieves a goal. No matter if it's a small one. And the more goals you achieve on a regular basis, the more neural pathways in your brain get stronger. So the more regularly you achieve the goals you set the hit of dopamine will become stronger. So the trick to this is to set yourself very small, achievable goals every day, and actually achieve them for regular hits of dopamine.

Ways to increase Dopamine:

- Get enough sleep
- Listen to music
- Maintain a healthy diet
- Exercise more
- Meditate
- Try something new
- Do something creative
- Achieve a goal

OXYTOCIN

The Love Hormone

Oxytocin "the love hormone" increases empathic feelings and also builds trust. The obvious way of getting more of this is sex, but the not-so-obvious ways are holding hands and cuddling. Or petting your cat!

Ways to increase Oxytocin:

- Play with a pet
- Hug someone you love
- Do something nice for someone
- Spend time with friends
- Show affection
- Give someone a compliment
- Holding hands

SEROTONIN

For Good Moods

Serotonin can be increased by being outside in bright daylight. Daylight is a standard treatment for seasonal depression. It's important to remember that 90% of serotonin is formed in your gut. So if you have a healthy gut, you'll have a lot of serotonin. This also makes the fact that if you're hungry, you can get angrier – a real thing!

Ways to increase Serotonin:

- Walk in nature
- Enjoy the sunshine
- Try yoga and meditation
- Swimming

Eat a healthy meal

ENDORPHINS

The Pain Reliever

Endorphins are your body's natural painkillers. And they also regulate the fight or flight instinct. So the obvious one for producing endorphins is exercise. But endorphins can be produced in many ways. For example, doing something you find scary will flood your body with endorphins. Even something as simple as watching a scary movie can fill your body with endorphins – or eating spicy food!

Ways to increase Endorphins:

- Laughter
- Essential Oils
- Dark Chocolate
- Running or walking
- Exercise
- Watch a movie

CHAPTER THIRTY-NINE

# Logical Vs Creative

**Logical Vs Creative**

You can't be logical & creative at the same time. your brain and mind are using different faculties and different abilities.

To do different types of tasks imagine you are in a meeting all-day about numbers and data and analytics and all of sudden, you are asked to do something creative maybe write a speech or give a presentation it can be really really difficult to switch from one side of your brain to the other side in a matter of seconds with very little organizing and planning.

we are literally going like a pendulum swinging from one task to another which is requiring different parts of our brain and the abilities that we have the way.

Start every day by first writing down your to-do list. looking at the activities that you have to do now.
I have simplified my task to make it easier. Draw a line down and the middle of the page on one side of it write logical and on another side of it write creative. you now want to plot and mark where these tasks on your to-do list fit either in the logical category or in the creative category the question you are asking yourself is whether the task is largely structured focused does it have certain boundaries is it quite a logical step by step process or is this creative is it more of a brainstorm?

Is it somewhere where you need to feel free and expressive? after you have divided these tasks. you now want to write down the time estimate that that specific task is going to take what ends up happening is you start to plot. Your week by saying Mondays are going to be creative Tuesdays are logical Wednesdays are logical Thursdays are creative and Fridays are creative or you may also divide your day up into logical mornings and creative afternoons or creative mornings
and logical afternoons this division this time blocking allows you to get really immersed into the activity really focus and be more productive and effective.

CHAPTER FORTY

# Priming Technique

Priming is the act of taking time to adjust your thoughts and emotions so you can live your life in your peak state. Priming is most powerful when completed in the morning to set a productive and powerful tone for your day. It's also useful for mastering your emotions as it gives you a moment to take a breath and control your reaction.

**1. SIT**

Find a chair in a relatively quiet area and sit actively. Place both feet on the floor, shift your shoulders back, chest up, and hold your neck long and your head high.

**2. BREATHE**

By changing your breath, you change your state of being. Tony's method incorporates a breathing exercise with three sets of 30 breaths, with a pause in between each set. 1 MINUTE

**3. BEGIN HEART BREATHING**

Put your hands on your heart. Feel its power and strength as you breathe into it. 30 SECONDS

**4. PRACTICE GRATITUDE**

Think of three things you're really grateful for right now. They can be from your past, present or future. Step into the first moment and picture it as vividly as possible. After about a minute, go to the second thing, then to the next.

**Pro tip:** Make one of these things simple, like a child's smile or a time someone said, "thank you" and really meant it. Even on your worst days, you can find something small and meaningful to be grateful for. 3 MINUTES

**5. VISUALIZE**

Now comes the part that's like a blessing or a prayer. It can be as spiritual as you want it to be. Tony imagines colorful light coming down and filling his body, healing anything that needs to be healed – body, thoughts, emotions, feelings. Envision your problems being washed away. Ask for the best parts of you to be strengthened. 1 MINUTE AND 30 SECONDS

**6. SHARE**

Now send all the energy you've gotten through your healing and strengthening out to others. Feel the energy going up and down, pouring out to your family, loved ones, colleagues, clients, friends, and even strangers you've only met once. 1 MINUTE AND 30 SECONDS

**7. FOCUS AND CELEBRATE**

Now think about the three outcomes or goals that you want to achieve the most. These are things that will excite you once they're completed. What would achieving them feel like? Place yourself in that position of achievement and celebrate that feeling of completion and victory. Visualize how it will impact you and what those victories could do for those around you. As with gratitude, go through each outcome one by one, fully experiencing the feeling of success. 3 MINUTES

**8. GET READY TO ROCK**

Take as long as you'd like to stretch and reflect on all of the positive work you just did. You are now positioned to excel in the state of your optimal self. Stay in character and get out there to conquer the day.

Printed by Libri Plureos GmbH in Hamburg,
Germany